Fact Finders™

~ The American Colonies ~

The New York Colony

by Martin Hintz

Consultant:
Timothy J. Shannon, Associate Professor of History
Gettysburg College
Gettysburg, Pennsylvania

Capstone press
Mankato, Minnesota

Fact Finders is published by Capstone Press,
151 Good Counsel Drive, P.O. Box 669, Mankato, Minnesota 56002.
www.capstonepress.com

Library of Congress Cataloging-in-Publication Data
Hintz, Martin.
    The New York colony / by Martin Hintz.
    p. cm.—(Fact Finders. The American colonies)
    Includes bibliographical references and index.
    ISBN-13: 978-0-7368-2679-2 (hardcover)
    ISBN-10: 0-7368-2679-3 (hardcover)
    ISBN-13: 978-0-7368-6102-1 (softcover pbk.)
    ISBN-10: 0-7368-6102-5 (softcover pbk.)
    1. New York (State)—History—Colonial period, ca. 1600–1775—Juvenile literature.
I. Title. II. American colonies (Capstone Press)
F122.H56 2006
974.7'02—dc22
                                      2005000123

Summary: An introduction to the history, government, economy, resources, and people of
    the New York Colony. Includes maps and charts.

Editorial Credits
Katy Kudela, editor; Jennifer Bergstrom, set designer, illustrator, and book designer;
    Bobbi J. Dey, book designer; Jo Miller, photo researcher/photo editor

Photo Credits
Cover image: View of the waterfront in New York City in the 1700s, The Granger
    Collection, New York

Corbis/Bettmann, 20–21
The Granger Collection, New York, 6, 10–11, 12–13, 14, 15, 18, 26, 27, 29 (left)
National Archives and Records Administration, 29 (right)
North Wind Picture Archives, 23
Stock Montage Inc., 5
SuperStock, 16–17

1 2 3 4 5 6 10 09 08 07 06 05

Table of Contents

Chapter 1

New York's First People

In the early 1600s, European explorers were excited to arrive in what would later become New York. But the explorers were not the first to discover this land. American Indians were already living there.

Iroquois People

The Iroquois were one of the largest Indian groups in New York. They were divided into five nations. These nations were the Cayuga, Mohawk, Oneida, Seneca, and Onondaga. Each of these nations split into groups called **clans**.

The Iroquois called themselves the people of the longhouse. They lived in longhouses built from cedar and elm trees.

The Iroquois lived in longhouse villages.

5

▲ The Iroquois dried and ground corn to make flour for bread.

The Iroquois got food from the land around them. They hunted animals in the forests and fished from rivers. They also cleared land for farming. They planted crops of corn, beans, and squash.

Iroquois women held positions of power. The women owned all the property. They also chose the tribal leaders.

FACT!

A longhouse could be as long as a football field. Several families lived together in one longhouse.

Early Trade

The Iroquois traded with European explorers. They exchanged animal furs for goods from Europe. Soon, battles over land ended the friendly trade between the two groups. By the late 1700s, many of the Iroquois moved out of New York.

Fur Trade in New York

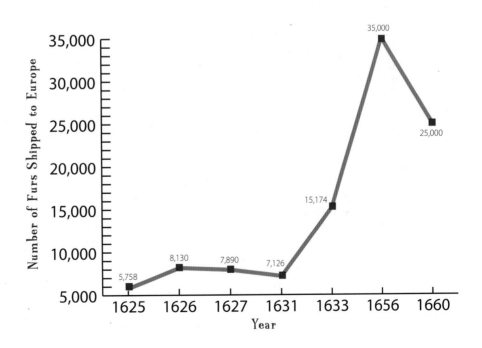

Chapter 2

Early Settlers

In 1609, Dutch **merchants** hired English explorer Henry Hudson to sail across the Atlantic Ocean. They hoped Hudson would find a sea passage to Asia. They wanted him to bring silk and other goods back from Asia.

After many days at sea, Hudson's ship landed at what is now New York. Following a month of searching, Hudson and his men did not find a shortcut to Asia. They returned to Europe.

The Dutch claimed the land Hudson explored. The land included what is today New York, New Jersey, Delaware, and parts of Connecticut. The Dutch began to build trading posts and villages there.

Early settlers built the New York Colony along the Hudson River. By 1763, the colony's borders had grown farther west. ➤

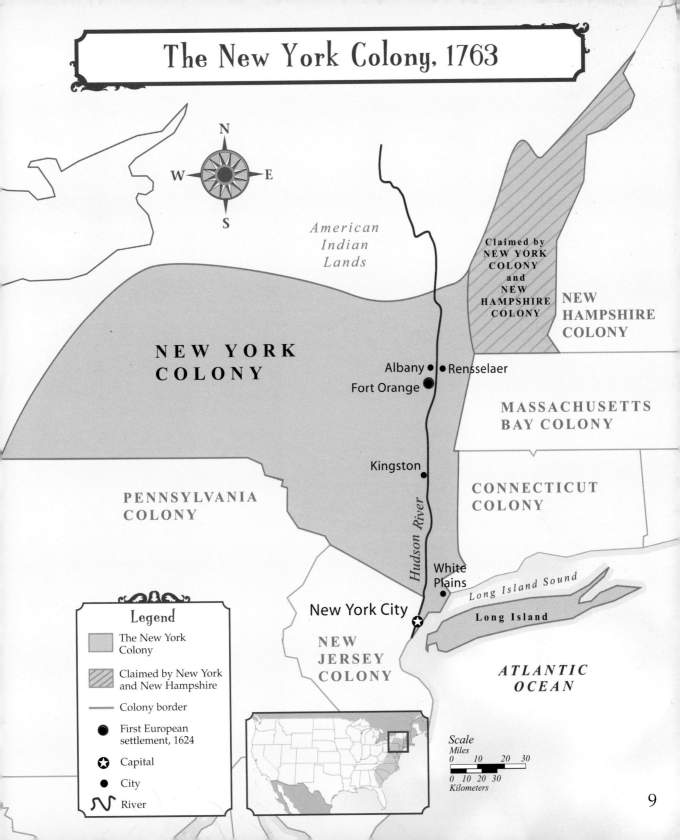

The New York Colony, 1763

American Indian Lands

Claimed by NEW YORK COLONY and NEW HAMPSHIRE COLONY

NEW HAMPSHIRE COLONY

NEW YORK COLONY

Albany • • Rensselaer
Fort Orange •

MASSACHUSETTS BAY COLONY

Kingston •

CONNECTICUT COLONY

PENNSYLVANIA COLONY

Hudson River

White Plains •

Long Island Sound

New York City ☆

Long Island

NEW JERSEY COLONY

ATLANTIC OCEAN

Legend

The New York Colony

Claimed by New York and New Hampshire

Colony border

● First European settlement, 1624

☆ Capital

● City

〰 River

Scale
Miles
0   10   20   30

0 10 20 30
Kilometers

New Netherland

In 1621, a group of merchants started the Dutch West India Company. The merchants hoped to gain riches in North America. Dutch leaders gave the company a **charter** for land in North America. They created a colony called New Netherland.

The company sent a ship of settlers to New Netherland in 1624. They built a trading post called Fort Orange. The next year, they built New Amsterdam. This settlement later became New York City.

Manhattan Island became part of the New Netherland colony in 1626. The colony's governor bought the land from the American Indians. He paid for the land with beads, cloth, and other small items.

Change of Power

Dutch rule did not last. In 1664, England took over the colony. The English let the Dutch stay. But they asked the Dutch colonists to swear loyalty to the English king. England renamed the colony New York after the Duke of York.

◀ The Dutch bought Manhattan Island from the American Indians for items worth only $24.

~ Chapter 3 ~
Colonial Life

From its beginning, people from many countries lived in New York. The colony's early settlers were Dutch, French, German, English, and Swedish. People from Africa were shipped to the colony and sold as slaves. They were put to work on farms and in rich households.

Most settlers lived within a day's journey of a town. Small farms and lone cabins were scattered along the Hudson River valley. Forests separated the settlers' orchards and fields. Settlers sailed boats on the rivers to carry goods to market.

Many New York colonists lived on small farms.

People from many countries settled in New York. By 1664, records say 18 different languages were spoken in the colony.

Young boys helped their fathers with fieldwork. ▼

Work for Everyone

On farms, everyone helped with the work. Children milked cows and collected eggs. Boys usually worked in the fields with their fathers. Girls helped cook meals, clean house, and take care of gardens.

On the **frontier**, settlers lived farther away from people and towns. Settlers had to rely on themselves for many goods. They grew their own crops and made their own butter. They also used animal skins to make leather for clothing and harnesses for horses.

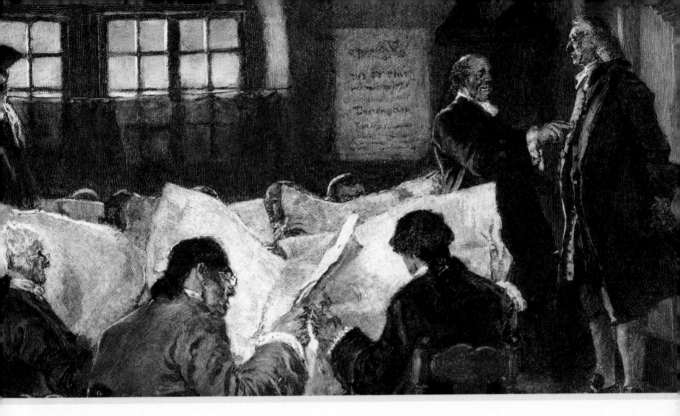

▲ New York City had coffeehouses where people could visit and read newspapers.

Schools

In the beginning, New York children spent little time in school. They were busy with work. People believed starting a colony was more important than starting schools. Gradually, the colonists built schools. In time, more children went to school and learned to read. By 1750, many colonists could read the newspaper and the Bible.

Chapter 4

Work and Trade

The New York Colony was full of businesses. Shops lined the streets of the cities and towns. Colonists made wooden barrels and leather boots. They brewed beer and baked bread.

In the country, farmers raised extra food for market. Colonists traded eggs, milk, and grain for goods they could not make or grow. Farmers also exchanged bushels of wheat, dried beef, and salted pork for items from Europe.

Colonists shipped many of their goods from New York City to Europe. The city quickly became a trading center for the American colonies.

New York City's port was a busy trading center in North America.

Early Dutch settlers started fur trading businesses with the American Indians.

Fur Trade

Many colonists in New York became rich in the fur business. They traded with the American Indians for animal furs. The furs were sold in Europe.

The city of Albany was a center for the fur trade. Its location along the Hudson River made it a busy river port.

Unpaid Workers

Wealthy colonists had people to help them with their work. Slaves often did household chores. The colonists also used the help of other workers, such as **indentured servants**. These servants worked to pay the debt of their trip to the colony. They worked for a fixed number of years.

FACT!

The New York fur trade was big business. In 1699, 15,000 furs were sent just from New York to England.

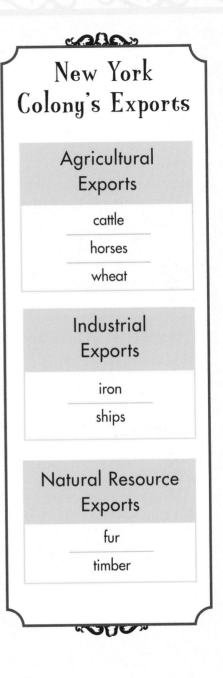

New York Colony's Exports

Agricultural Exports

cattle

horses

wheat

Industrial Exports

iron

ships

Natural Resource Exports

fur

timber

Chapter 5

Community and Faith

People of many religions were welcomed in New York. Most of the early settlers belonged to the Dutch Reformed Church. Under England's rule, many colonists were Anglicans. They followed the Church of England.

Religious Freedom

Unlike some colonies, New York did not make rules about religion. Many groups settled and even built their own towns. Many Lutherans settled west of Albany. Meanwhile, the French Huguenots built a town just north of New York City.

Colonists in New York were free to attend the church of their choice.

In New York, people found the
land and the religious freedom they
wanted. Jewish colonists built their
first **synagogue** in New York in 1730.
Catholics and followers of other religions
also built churches and practiced
their faiths.

Population Growth of the New York Colony

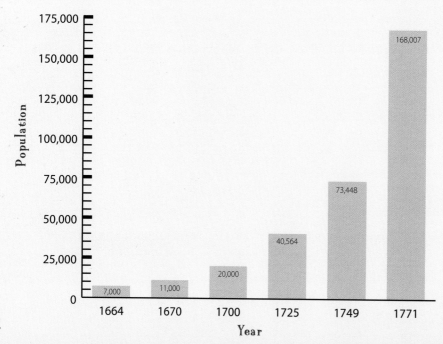

Colonists Speak Out

New York colonists valued freedom of speech. In 1735, John Peter Zenger went to jail for printing articles about the governor in his newspaper. These articles had upset the governor. Zenger's case went to trial. The jurors in New York believed people should be able to speak the truth. They freed Zenger from jail.

This court case became an important decision. Freedom of speech remains a basic right in the United States today.

John Peter Zenger's court case showed the importance of freedom of speech. ➡

Chapter 6

Becoming a State

During the late 1600s, France became interested in claiming land in northern New York. Around this same time, war broke out between Great Britain and France. The two countries began to fight over land in North America.

Great Britain and France fought the French and Indian wars (1689–1763). American Indian groups also helped fight these wars. Some Indians helped the French, some aided the British, and some did not take sides.

Great Britain defeated the French in 1763. The win over France came at a great cost. The British army and navy had to be paid.

New York was the most northern of the middle colonies. ➡

The Thirteen Colonies, 1763

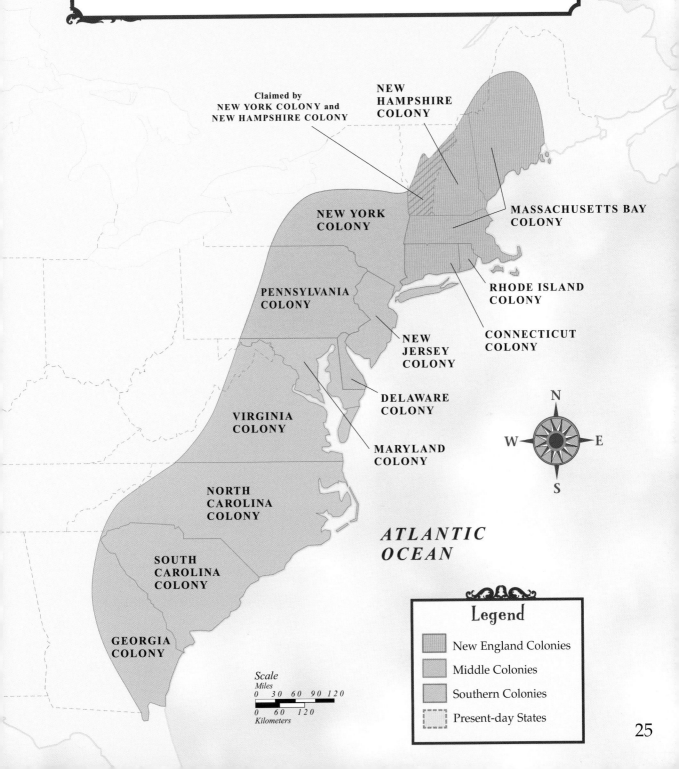

Claimed by
NEW YORK COLONY and
NEW HAMPSHIRE COLONY

NEW HAMPSHIRE COLONY

NEW YORK COLONY

MASSACHUSETTS BAY COLONY

PENNSYLVANIA COLONY

RHODE ISLAND COLONY

CONNECTICUT COLONY

NEW JERSEY COLONY

DELAWARE COLONY

VIRGINIA COLONY

MARYLAND COLONY

NORTH CAROLINA COLONY

SOUTH CAROLINA COLONY

GEORGIA COLONY

ATLANTIC OCEAN

N
W   E
S

Scale
Miles
0   30   60   90 120
0   60   120
Kilometers

Legend
- New England Colonies
- Middle Colonies
- Southern Colonies
- Present-day States

Following the war, Great Britain placed many taxes on the colonies. Britain's heavy taxes were one of the causes of the Revolutionary War. The colonies fought Britain from 1775 to 1783.

At the start of the war, Great Britain took control of New York City. Many colonists who supported the king lived in the city. British soldiers kept these Loyalists safe. The colonists living on the frontier were not safe. British soldiers and some American Indians attacked farms and villages.

Angry colonists in New York burned papers in protest of British taxes.

Independence

In July 1776, Continental Congress approved the Declaration of Independence. This document declared the colonies free from Great Britain. The war continued for seven more years. In 1783, the United States finally won.

After winning the war, the American states formed a stronger national government. Representatives wrote a plan for the government. On July 26, 1788, New York approved the **Constitution** of the United States. New York was the 11th state to join the United States.

After the British left New York City in 1783, the citizens of the new nation raised the American flag. ➡

Fast Facts

Name

The New York Colony
(named for the Duke of York)

Location

Middle colonies

Year of Founding

1624

First Settlement

Fort Orange

Colony's Founders

Dutch West India Company

Religious Faiths

Catholic, Church of England,
Dutch Reformed, French
Huguenot, Jewish, Protestant

Agricultural Products

Cattle, horses, wheat

Major Industries

Fur trade, logging, shipbuilding

Population in 1771

168,007 people

Statehood

July 26, 1788
(11th state)

Time Line

1600s ————————————————————— 1700s

1626
Manhattan Island becomes part of New Netherland.

1689-1763
Great Britain and France fight over land in North America; these wars are called the French and Indian wars.

1776
Declaration of Independence is approved in July.

1707
An Act of Union unites England, Wales, and Scotland; they become the Kingdom of Great Britain.

1624
Dutch settlers build the first settlement in New Netherland.

1788
On July 26, New York is the 11th state to join the United States.

1664
England takes control of the Dutch colony.

1763
Proclamation of 1763 sets colonial borders and provides land for American Indians.

1775-1783
American colonies fight for their independence from Great Britain in the Revolutionary War.

1609
Henry Hudson sails to North America.

29

Glossary

charter (CHAR-tur)—an official document that grants permission to create a city or colony and provides for a government

clan (KLAN)—a large group of related families

constitution (kon-stuh-TOO-shuhn)—the written system of laws in a state or country that state the rights of the people and the powers of the government

frontier (fruhn-TIHR)—an undeveloped area where few people live

indentured servant (in-DEN-churd SUR-vuhnt)—someone who agrees to work for another person for a certain length of time in exchange for travel expenses, food, or housing

merchant (MUR-chuhnt)—someone who sells goods to others, such as a store owner

synagogue (SIN-a-gog)—a building where Jewish people come together to pray